HANNAH SPARKLES

A FRIEND THROUGH RAIN OR SHINE

By
Robin Mellom

Illustrated by
Vanessa Brantley-Newton

HARPER
An Imprint of HarperCollinsPublishers

For L.M.—the sparkle is strong with you —R.M.

To my sisters and friends Coy and Wendy,
with love —V.B.N.

Hannah Sparkles: A Friend Through Rain or Shine
Text copyright © 2017 by Robin Mellom
Illustrations copyright © 2017 by Vanessa Brantley-Newton
All rights reserved. Manufactured in China.
No part of this book may be used or reproduced in any manner whatsoever without written
permission except in the case of brief quotations embodied in critical articles and reviews.
For information address HarperCollins Children's Books, a division of HarperCollins Publishers,
195 Broadway, New York, NY 10007.
www.harpercollinschildrens.com

Library of Congress Cataloging-in-Publication Data
Mellom, Robin.
    Hannah Sparkles / by Robin Mellom ; illustrated by Vanessa Brantley-Newton. — First edition.
        pages   cm
    Summary: "Hannah Sparkles, an enthusiastic little girl who loves life and pom-poms, learns
that everyone finds happiness in different ways" — Provided by publisher.
    ISBN 978-0-06-232233-3 (hardcover)
    [1. Happiness—Fiction.   2. Individuality—Fiction.]   I. Brantley-Newton, Vanessa,
illustrator.   II. Title.
PZ7.M16254Han   2016   2015015556
[E]—dc23   CIP
                                                                                  AC

The artwork for this book was created by hand sketching, Photoshop, and Corel Painter 12.
Typography by Whitney Manger
17 18 19 20 21   SCP   10 9 8 7 6 5 4 3 2 1
❖
First Edition

The story goes . . . I was born happy. I didn't cry one bit.
Smiled all the time, my parents say. Even in my sleep.

They say I *still* smile in my sleep.
My parents are proud. See their proud faces?

To me, smiling is necessary.
Also necessary? Pom-poms.

Pom-poms are the best way
to show excitement.

TWIRL,
SPARKLE,
SHINE!

I share my sparkle at breakfast. *Totally delicious!*

And in the car.
Excellent left turn, Mom!

And when dessert arrives. *Nice presentation!*

Ugh, I may have overdone it.

When I'm not cheering with pom-poms, you might find me drawing. Happy drawings, of course.

Today, I was in my room making a double rainbow. (Because why stop at one, right?) Mom stuck her head in. "I have some news, Hannah."

This was perfect. *I love news!*

"We have new neighbors," my mom said. "Their
daughter is your age. Her name is Sunny Everbright."

A girl. My age. Next door. And her name is Sunny Everbright?
That's the happiest name ever! This is better than a pet unicorn!

I couldn't wait to introduce myself! I even left my pom-poms behind. THAT'S how excited I was.

I flashed a friendly smile and
knocked out a happy beat on
her door.

"Hi, I'm Hannah. Welcome to the neighborhood."

"Do you like riding bikes?"

"No."

"Finding butterflies?"

"No."

"Drawing unicorns?"

"No."

I was worried. Maybe her teacher had only taught her one word.

But I had a final idea that she wouldn't be able to resist.
"I've got it! How about leaving flowers in the mailbox
for the mail carrier?"

"No thanks."

I wasn't sure what to do. But then it hit me. . . .

PROJECT!

I knew it right then and there. If we were going to be friends, I would have to teach Sunny Everbright how to be happy. It was time for her to

SPARKLE.

We started off slowly.
"For drawing hearts, magenta
is your go-to color."

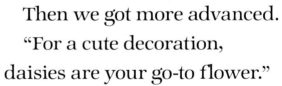

Then we got more advanced.
"For a cute decoration,
daisies are your go-to flower."

And then . . . super-advanced.
"If you need a smile, the strawberry
is your go-to fruit."

Nothing was working. I knew there was one thing that couldn't possibly fail.

Pom-poms and a happy cheer.

SLIDE,

SPARKLE,

SHINE!

FLIP, SPARKLE, SHINE!

SKIP, SPARKLE, SHINE!

But I just couldn't seem to get Sunny to smile.

And then it happened. Rain. Lots of it.
I will admit—I am not good with rain. It does not make me
happy. Everything gets so . . . *wet*. And droopy. And soggy.

But Sunny did the strangest thing.

Then even stranger.

And then . . . super-strange.

I couldn't figure out how to get Sunny to be my friend. She didn't like all the things that make me happy. I wasn't feeling sparkly inside—not even one little spark.

That night I told my mom, "I don't understand Sunny. Why don't all my favorite things make her smile?"

"We all find happiness in different ways, Hannah. Maybe Sunny finds her sparkle in other things."

I perked up at this. "Like rain? Or mud? Or *LIZARDS*?"

My mom hugged me tightly. "Exactly, Hannah. Even lizards."

And guess what? The next morning, I found out my mom was right.

Sunny had her own kind of sparkle!

SHINE!

I have a feeling the two of us will always
be friends . . . through rain or shine.